WHITE FRAGILITY

Summarized for Busy People

Why It's So Hard for White People to Talk About
Racism

Based on the Book by Robin J. DiAngelo

Goldmine Reads

Copyright © Goldmine Reads

TABLE OF CONTENT

ABOUT THE AUTHOR

An American academic, educator and author, White Fragility's author, Robin J. DiAngelo specializes in critical discourse analysis and whiteness studies. During the course of her career, she has published two other books; both of which are centered on social justice and racial equality. She has been a two-time recipient of the Student's Choice Awards for Educator of the Year.

Currently residing in Seattle, Washington, DiAngelo has been a consultant and trainer on topics involving racial issues for over twenty years. She completed a Ph.D. degree in Multicultural Education at the Washington University. Following her academic accomplishment, she then went on to pursue a career at the Westfield State University—first as a lecturer in 2007, and then as a multicultural education professor in 2014. At present, she is now a part-time lecturer at Washington University's School of Social Work. Aside from lecturing part-time at Washington University, DiAngelo is also the Equity Director of Sound Generations, a Seattle-based non-profit organization.

DiAngelo is also known and respected for her seminars and workshop about racial issues. She discusses how American politics and culture has been deeply embedded with racism. In 2011, she formulated the term "white fragility". It was after she wrote her thesis, one that was also reviewed by peers. Major publications that featured DiAngelo's article include the Atlantic, Colorlines, the New York Times and Salon.

ABOUT THIS BOOK SUMMARY

This book summary and analysis was created for individuals who want to extract the essential contents and are too busy to go through the full version.

With the aid of this summary, readers will find it easier to digest the terminologies and concepts introduced by the author in White Fragility. All of the sensitive topics tackled in explaining the negative involvement of white individuals in reinforcing racism are introduced in a manner that readers will focus more on the intellectual aspect of the book's content rather the emotional affect that it instigates. This way, the audience can go through each of the chapter's fundamental principles with a more critical eye, and readily do self reflections as they read further into the book.

This book is not intended to replace the original copy. We highly encourage you to purchase the full version instead.

BOOK OVERVIEW

Robin J. DiAngelo's book, White Fragility: Why It's So Hard for White People to Talk about Racism, delves deep into the notion that white Americans are socially built to keep their mouths zipped when it comes to issues involving racism. It is this social construct that restrains their capability to bear with any conversation or argument that's centered on racial justice and equality. Their inhibition leaves white individuals aggressive and on defense whenever their racist beliefs are being confronted openly.

The term 'white fragility' is describe as "a condition wherein even just the smallest level of racial stress becomes unbearable, thus prompting an array of self-protective responses." A white person would usually become reserved or assertive whenever their ideas and statements that are racist in nature are questioned. Where the problem lies in this is that, white people are consumed by the belief that an evil individual is the one behind racist events and behavior. But that is not really the case.

The truth is racism is an organization and structure encompassing every aspect of American culture and society. In fact, white individuals are this structure's silent recipients. Put more simply, a person can be good yet still hold racially prejudiced perspectives. The author argues that even without them realizing it, white people frequently exercise this.

DiAngelo proposes that it is necessary for white people to learn how to not be indifferent and overprotective while trying to put up with conversations that tackle racism. More importantly, white people must also take an in-depth examination of their life choices and work to confront their racially discriminative ideas and views.

CHAPTER 1: WHY IS IT CHALLENGING TO DISCUSS RACISM WITH WHITE PEOPLE?

In the first chapter of her book, DiAngelo focuses on the main hurdles she is confronted with every time she tries to persuade white people to discuss racism. She specifies that there are four main issues or topics that white people tend to go to whenever a question about race is aimed at them. According to the author, the way the definition of what it means to be a "racist" is simplified, followed by uneducated opinions, socialization and race identity are the challenges of discussing racism topics.

Being a white person herself, DiAngelo identifies that her frame of reference, life experiences and perspective of the world are all fundamentally white in nature. She also contends that just like every other white individual, she was brought up with the idea of discounting the color of her skin along with the implication that she should not take advantage of her race to get ahead in life. It is this manner of child rearing and development that make white people discuss issues involving race only on rare occasions.

Despite that, race remains to be a major issue in American society. This is because of the presence of a deep-seated inequality on race. The author adds that if this particular racial inequality is to be addressed, then white people must behave as though race is a big deal. That being said, a white person must "name or identify what their race is" no matter how awkward it may feel to them.

DiAngelo shares how all the white people she has met in her life carry with them strong perspectives on racism. On the other hand, she asserts that because white people rely on information that is biased against people of color, their opinions on race are more often than not, uninformed or uneducated. To top it off, the culture and media representing Mainstream American society is overflowing with social authorities consistently trying to force a particular account about being racist.

Each time the topic of racism is raised, the usual response of white people is to either keep silent or put up a defense and start an argument. These types of responses keep white people from gaining a more comprehensive and wider understanding about issues concerning race. As a result, the structure of a racist mindset continues to be reinforced.

The pattern or type of response holds true even when white people are asked about racism—a consequence of their shared socialization and culture. Individuality and objectivity are the two ideologies that hold back white people from realizing how their racial perspectives are being blocked by their cultural and societal upbringing.

People in the Western area are taught the belief that their individual personality bears more significance than the group where they are thriving socially. If individuals are the architects of racial discrimination and injustice, then it should not be deemed as a problem by another individual. DiAngelo counters this thought process by insisting that racism is a problem that involves groups of individuals. Here's an example: On a subconscious level, children are being trained to think and believe that there are groups better than the others, making it ideal or preferable for them to be in the group with the most advantage or favor. Another negating ideology that has been taught to white people is that it is biased to have an opinion of racism. Since it is biased, then white people choose to not reflect on their standpoints. In reality, racism cannot be understood by a person if they turn down the chance to learn more about how the culture of a group can influence individuals.

Majority of individuals automatically assume that when a person is racist, they lack morals and they use race as their basis for being spiteful on other people. White people don't really identify with this particular definition of what being a racist is, and that is why they would usually oppose people who accuse them of being one. According to the author, this definition of a racist is erroneous. The key to conquering white fragility lies in the acceptance of white people on the distress coupled with learning the true meaning of racism.

CHAPTER 2: RACISM AND THE SUPERIORITY OF WHITE PEOPLE

Races may be different, but all are essentially the same biologically and genetically speaking. The differences of each race in terms of their eye, hair and skin color are the result of how their physical bodies have adapted to their geographical location. This means that, similar to gender, race is a social concept.

DiAngelo expounds on how both social and economic influences continuously work together to keep society on opposite sides of the fence when it comes to topics and discussions about race.

While America may be built on the standards if equality and freedom, the country's economy was built on three major events in history that contradict is two founding principles. From the slavery of the Africans to the genocide of Native Americans to the invasion of Mexico, all of these tragic and inhumane events form the American economy. Scientists even went as far as to attempt to create an excuse for the Americans' unjust treatment of people of color. Scientists argued that people of color were naturally of lesser worth and class compared to white people. A narrative of the genetic inferiority of black individuals was devised to redirect the focus and attention of people away from the full discrimination being practiced by white people.

Following the mass immigration of Europeans to America, Armenians, Irish, Italians and Polish were strangely not categorized or grouped with white people. They had to raise a petition to courts wherein men who were identified as white grouped individuals and races by judging on whether these people are white or not.

The primarily social concept of race made people's social status complicated. White Americans who were poor were considered to be citizens belonging to the second-class. Full whiteness was then granted to whites belonging to the working-class to prevent them from starting a dispute against the top elite of the social ranks. The elites figured out that for as long as the working class were more fixated on feeling superior over people of color, then they would no longer complain about their poverty's true root cause.

Discrimination, prejudice and racism are three different things: Discrimination is done to reinforce prejudice, or the act of presupposing certain expectations and ideas about others based on the social group where they belong. Meanwhile, racism is explained as a system that is backed by legal, social and institutional authorities and influences.

White people in the US possess control over all power tools and resources. Their exclusive access to such resources makes them more empowered to practice their racial advantage over other races, especially in their country. On the contrary, people of color lack the policies and laws that enable them to apply societal discrimination, despite their prejudice against white people.

CHAPTER 3: HOW RACISM CHANGED AFTER THE CIVIL RIGHTS MOVEMENT

Contrary to what white Americans believe, racism is still very much alive, albeit in a more implied form that has adapted throughout the times and the changing standards and views of society. This chapter focuses on the drastic change in racism and how present-day white individuals no longer feel a strong sense of participation in the domineering system of racism.

DiAngelo adds that there is a phenomenon called color-blind racism. It takes place when a person chooses to ignore the presence of racism by acting as if they are clueless about the skin color of a person who is not white. Back in the time of the Civil Rights movement, the white people were astonished when they witnessed the brutal treatment of black people. Following the King's renowned speech, several white people made the assumption that, as long as an individual's race was not acknowledged or recognized by white people, then it would inevitably put an end on racism.

Sadly, when a person pretends not to see or recognize color, they are only projecting their own version of reality to the other party. An example of this is when a white person is receiving good treatment at work and assumes that all his colleagues of color are the same. When a person has color blind racism, they become unable to tackle the negative and insensible notions about other racial backgrounds.

DiAngelo likewise shares a personal experience of witnessing racism from her peers and co-workers. They mentioned specific areas and locations where she was not advised to get a house. According to her co-workers and friends, these areas were unsafe or had little security. Upon further investigation, DiAngelo discovered that all the areas that they mentioned had mainly black and brown people as residents. For DiAngelo, what her friends and colleagues did is an example of aversive racism.

Aversive racism is when coded language is being used by white individuals to make statements that are racist even without sounding racist on the surface. Since it is subtle, it makes for helping a person preserve a favorable image about their self.

Even millennials are still exhibiting racism, DiAngelo explicates. There are white college students who, when surrounded by all-white companions, would make deliberate racist comments yet when they see that there are people of color near the area, they suddenly become racially mindful. There have been studies that proved how racism is already embedded in white individuals during their childhood days. As such, millennials are no different from the older generations in being racist.

CHAPTER 4: WHAT IS THE ROLE AND INFLUENCEOF RACE IN SHAPING WHITE PEOPLE'S LIVES?

What is the reason behind the discomfort of white people whenever the topic of race is raised? In the fourth chapter, DiAngelo discloses the factors that serve as the foundations of white fragility. These factors are only applicable to those who do not fall into the classification of people of color.

Here is a concrete scenario: A child, who is of white descent, is born. The child is reared and grows up bearing the thought that they belong to the more superior or prevailing group in the society. This is an assumption they pick up from the things they observe around them during their day-to-day encounters: Their favorite books are written by white authors, their school has predominantly white teachers and the hospitals with the best reputations are run mostly by white doctors. Since they are surrounded by people with the same skin color as theirs', they feel belongingness as something natural, never finding any issue about it until such time that they encounter or get associated with a person of color.

Unless a white person is in attendance of a gathering or event organized by people of color, they will not worry or stress about their skin color. They will not think twice about what other people will make out and say about the color of their skin.

They can pursue any hobby and career they want and engage in any activity of their choice without being hampered by their physical appearance. Another argument that DiAngelo uses to make her point more concrete, is the fact that George Zimmerman would never stop nor shoot a white person. Zimmerman was the person responsible for the murder of the 17-year-old African-American teen, Trayvon Martin in 2012.

White people can go wherever they want and move to wherever place they want. In contrast, the author shares how about one of her associates who happened to be of color. This associate of hers often avoided going to northern Idaho for the holidays, because of the Aryan Nation that lived and camped at the said location. Her associate likewise added that she fears the white people in northern Idaho may not have any experience mingling with a person of color and would thus, segregate her.

CHAPTER 5: THE DUALITY OF WHAT IS GOOD AND BAD

There is a term in White Fragility called good/bad binary. It is a variation of racism that recently emerged. In all honesty, white people did not have any issues with their racist ways, up until they reached the 1960s. Following the Civil Rights movement, racism was only viewed as an issue of immorality faced by whites in the southern part of the land. This notion led to the creation of the dyad that implies a moral or good individual cannot be racist.

This particular dichotomy is exemplified when a white person feels as though they are being personally attacked whenever they are called racist. They see it as an assault to their principles and character. According to DiAngelo, this kind of thinking is incorrect. Morality and racism are not equally exclusive. In other words, a person can be morally upright, yet still agree with social constructs that promote racist beliefs and actions. The more white individuals choose not to confront the faulty system, the more racism will prevail.

During one of her presentations, DiAngelo encountered a white teacher protesting against the structure of the school. The white teacher was obviously mocking an agitated black woman. The teacher ended up putting up a defense and leaving in the middle of the presentation when she was confronted about her racial mockery.

The white teacher's behavior is a perfect example of how, in response to their racist actions and words being called out, white individuals tend to use certain behavioral responses and declarations in order to demonstrate that they are morally upright. Some of the most common statements said by racist white individuals to defend their character include:

- *I once lived as part of a minority group in Africa.*
- *I have colleagues/friends who are black.*
- *I was raised in a diverse but poor neighborhood.*

- *I don't have racist parents. Growing up, I was taught to treat people equally.*
- *The issue here is not about race.*
- *Discussing racism is what keeps people separated.*

The problem is that, the issue of racism stems from deep within the American society, making it harder for white people to see the truth with their naked eyes. All the aforementioned statements do not, in any way, prove that a white person's racially offensive words and acts are not racist.

CHAPTER 6: ANTI-BLACK MOVEMENT

America is rich with different cultures and ethnic backgrounds. It has been home to Asians, indigenous people, blacks and whites. Unfortunately, while there has already been a diverse racial background in America, white people see themselves as an exceptional group. In addition, all other people of color experience a certain level of racism. Sadly, blacks are what whites consider as something akin to the main "antagonist".

The author asserts that white individuals need to see themselves as a group that is socially constructed to be against black people.

DiAngelo adds the notion that white is, in fact, a false identity. What she meant is that, without any other race or group of color, "white" does not exist. Black people are being used by white people as a target for cohesive dislike and disapproval. It is this form of cohesive hatred that makes white people feel that they are superior among other races and groups of color. They build up a fake narrative just to create this imagery wherein they are above other races while black people sit at the most inferior part of this so-called societal hierarchy.

This made-up and insinuated hierarchy is what white people use to normalize their tendency to avoid people of color as well as justify black enslavement. Moreover, white people project their insecurities to black people. For example, despite how hard black people work in plantation farms, they are still labeled as aggressive and lazy and they are even made to suffer brutal attacks from white people.

The occurrence called "white flight", according to studies, take place whenever families of black people start moving into a neighborhood that is predominantly white in population. About 30% of blacks in the neighborhood are what majority of white Americans claim for them to be a tolerable amount of people of color within their vicinity. However, the numbers provided by white Americans is contradicted by actual movement patterns. Significant data from actual movement patterns show that once a neighborhood is comprised of as little as 7% black people, white individuals are already packing their bags and moving to a different town.

The American Sociological Foundation revealed in 2015 that in terms of racial preferences, whites are more in favor of Asians, followed by Latinos in their localities. Even more alarming is how the largest amount of segregation occurs between black people and white people.

White people are aware of the exploitation done by their ancestors to black people during the early parts of their history. Whites feel guilt and trauma over the wrongdoings of their ancestors, and they cope with the emotional distress by trying to rationalize the mistreatments inflicted on blacks. In their minds, they re-shaped the imagery of black people into non-human entities to make it easier to convince themselves that the brutality can be justified and that black people deserved the maltreatment they had to endure. Think of how white people choose to remain silent whenever blacks become the object of police brutality without just reasons, or how they are referred to in mainstream media as apes.

CHAPTER 7: WHAT TRIGGERS RACISM IN WHITE INDIVIDUALS?

Being white provides an individual with a number of privileges that involve resources and social status. These privileges often serve as a protective barrier for white people against different types of distress that involves racial issues. Seldom do white people take time to take into consideration racial issues. When they do, it is often in the context of workplace seminars and courses taken during their college years. As a result, white fragility is set off the moment whites are openly questioned about the realities of racial differences.

To further explain the main factors involved in explaining white fragility, DiAngelo uses a theory by Bourdieu. Capital, field and habitus are the three factors that the theory focuses on. Capital is the term used to describe a person's social value, while field depicts the social setting or context in which a person is present. Habitus refers to the consciousness that one has about their status, along with how they choose to react to other people's statuses. An example of a social value is how a receptionist is deemed to be of higher status than a janitor. Meanwhile, examples of field can be the neighborhood, office or school.

All three factors are dependent on social cues. These social cues are usually determined by those who possess the most social value or capital, and consequently followed by those who belong to the lower "ranks" with the amount of capital that they possess. During instances where an individual's social equilibrium is questioned, the automatic response is for the person to attempt to recover the stability of their social standing.

White people often take part in self-protective behavioral responses whenever they feel that their social balance is being attacked or disrupted. Exposure to racial stress is one of the most common ways that white people experience this. Aside from being overwhelmed by the feeling of guilt, white people also exhibit anger and apprehension, become confrontational, opt to stay silent or walk out of the conversation. In addition, the author clarifies that their behavioral responses are simply because they lack the knowledge of how to react to racial stress in a constructive manner. The end result is they exhibit Reponses that are impulsive and conventional in nature in order to retrieve what was lost in their capital.

CHAPTER 8: THE AFTERMATH OF WHITE FRAGILITY

Majority of white people are driven by the belief that in the present-day America, they are becoming the subject of prejudice and discrimination. However, only a handful of whites are able to testify that they have truly experienced being belittled or victimized. For instance, whenever people of color raise the issue of racial discrimination, white people retort in a manner that seems as though they were personally harassed by the said problem. Instead of acknowledging the concerns of people of color, they behave as if they were disturbed or distressed. Furthermore, whites will try to take control of the discussion and push for it to stop.

DiAngelo presses that this type of behavior is an example of white bullying.

Back in 2016, for the second year in a row, the Oscars failed to include black actors in their roster of nominees. The prestigious awards show was heavily criticized for its deliberate exclusion of black actors, an issue that some white actors deemed as discriminatory on their part. This response is an example of the self-protective manner that whites exhibit every time they are confronted with racial issues.

There have been some organizations in the past that have cautioned her about incidences where white individuals in the workplace have been significantly shocked after employers tried to broaden horizons in the work environment through the inclusion people with color. On one account, DiAngelo discloses that she was told a white woman was said to have had a heart attack following the way her racially discriminative statements left a negative impact on the people of color in their office.

Claims of trauma in what is supposed to be a diversified setting prevents the management from tackling deficiencies in implementing an inclusive work environment. When white people raise concerns of being traumatized, they are preventing racial issues from being challenged or questioned, thus enabling them to maintain their privilege. The management's attention is then refocused on a different problem, and racial issues remain unresolved and unacknowledged. In the end, white supremacy prevails in the work place.

It was pointed out by a sociological study that white people shift to a somehow unfathomable manner of speech every time they discuss issues involving race in public settings. From deviations and repetitions to long pauses in between phrases and sentences, to self-corrections, whites are reinforcing their belief that race is not as relevant as their colored counterparts insist it to be. It is also a clear manifestation of how unprepared they are to disclose their views on race.

In the end, the white perspective remains to be assumed as the universal viewpoint—for as long as white people are unwilling and hesitant to openly discuss about racism.

CHAPTER 9: WHITE FRAGILITY: DAILY DEMONSTRATIONS

The author enumerates concrete and relevant examples of the common reactions' whites portray in response to issues involving racial equality.

DiAngelo once questioned a woman named Eva, a white woman who cited that, having been raised in Germany with zero interaction with black people; she cannot be identified as racist. The author responded by asking her how she has interacted with blacks the moment she migrated to the U.S. She was also asked if she had seen films that feature African Americans.

After a while, DiAngelo was confronted by Eva. The latter expressed how she was enraged and insulted by DiAngelo's questions. Take note, no one—not even the author—had ever referred to her as racist. Based on this experience alone, the author has deduced that there is a specific patter being followed by white fragility.

Because of her upbringing, Eva assumed that she cannot be racist. In contrast, DiAngelo indicated that just because Eva grew up in an environment where she did not encounter black people, that does not automatically mean that she is incapable of harboring thoughts and opinions that are offensive to black individuals.

White fragility usually includes the following emotional responses:

- Accused
- Angry
- Attacked
- Guilty
- Insulted
- Judged

In the example involving Eva, Eva was driven by her emotions. On impulse, she portrayed a series of behavioral responses, all of which are also common in white fragility. Some of these include:

- Arguing

- Avoiding

- Crying

- Denying

- Physically leaving

- Seeking absolution

Following the aforementioned behavioral patterns, there are also specific claims that white people use to validate their emotional and behavioral responses. The goal of these claims is to prevent any more elaboration on racism or pinpointing of their liability.

Among the types of claims exhibited in white fragility are:

- "I'm aware of all this"

- "I didn't mean it that way"

- "I don't like/I don't feel comfortable with your tone"

- "I have friends who are black"

- "I've been misunderstood/misinterpreted"

- "I've suffered, too!"

- "My feelings have been hurt" / "You've offended my feelings

- "Race is not the problem, its class/gender/etc."

- "There are people who get insulted even though there isn't anything to be insulted about"

- "That's your own opinion"

- "You're the racist one"

The following, according to the author, are the purposes of white fragility:

- It portrays white people as the victims

- It preserves the advantages of whites

- It protects the cohesion among white individuals

- It blocks the practice of self-reflection

- It attacks the person who pointed out the racial statements/actions of white people, instead of the issue of racism

- It belittles the weight of racism as a real and prevailing problem in the society

Put simply, white fragility envelopes racist beliefs, opinions and behaviors in a protective barrier.

CHAPTER 10: WHITE FRAGILITY: ETIQUETTE IN DISCOURSE

DiAngelo's years of experience with training in diversity led to her discovery of the unspoken guidelines used by whites prior to the acceptance of comments about racial inequality. The implicit rules, as elaborated below, are crafted to conceal racism as it takes place and shield the superiority that white individuals hold.

The author has compiled white fragility's 11 unspoken rules:

1. No matter what happens, never offer or suggest opinions about my racist remarks and behavior – This is the most fundamental rule. If this rule is broken, the following guidelines must be followed strictly and accordingly.

2. Interact in a tone that is acceptable – Feedback and responses should be delivered in a calm manner. Any hint of emotional reaction will lead to a dismissal of the other party's opinions.

3. Trust should be mutual – Other people must assume or believe that whites are not racist before they even attempt to question the latter's racially offensive implications.

4. There should be no existing issues between the involved parties – It is important that whites and people who confront them about racist issues reconcile any prior and unrelated misunderstandings they may have between each other.

5. Feedback should be given quickly – If it takes too long for someone to give their opinion, then it will not be deemed of critical importance.

6. Regardless if the incident took place in a public setting, all feedback should be raised privately – Putting whites in a compromising spot discredits the other person's opinion about the white individual's racist behavior and/or statement. Thus, this makes the white person the victim in the situation.

7. Keep opinions and responses indirect – Direct responses are insensitive to the feelings of white individuals.

8. It is necessary that white people feel secure while discussing topics about race – White people will feel unsafe if someone remarks that they have racist assumptions. In order to rebuild the trust of whites, people should remember to quit challenging the racist tendencies of their white comrades.

9. Pointing out that a white person is racist nullifies the cruelties that they have endured – These cruelties include classism and sexism. Since whites have undergone oppression, questioning their racism is a form of discrimination for them as well.

10. It must be acknowledged that whites always carry good intentions – This must be the idea that people have about whites, despite their racist words and actions.

11. When people call a white person racist, that means that the white individual's words and actions were taken out of context – In other words, people should allow whites to elaborate on their viewpoint. Doing so will make their naysayers admit to their errors.

All 11 rules are highly effective in silencing any challenging opinions or questions that highlight the racist inclinations of whites. Some of the rules cited above are impracticable and clashing, DiAngelo adds.

CHAPTER 11: WHITE WOMEN SHED WHITE TEARS

There is a reference that depicts the methods that white people use to cry over how racism affects them. This reference is called 'white tears'. Specifically, DiAngelo identifies the way white women cry in places or setups with multiracial people. Each time these women shed tears, they are driving away attention from the racist issue that must be addressed at that point in time. Crying is also an effective way to turn the tables and make people of color appear to be the antagonists of a racially discriminative situation.

Citing yet again from her previous experiences, DiAngelo shares a cross-racial community meeting she attended in the past. The meeting was held following police fired the gun on a black man who was unarmed. A woman of color approached DiAngelo before the meeting. The woman told DiAngelo that she really wasn't looking forward to dealing with the "tears of white women", and therefore she is hesitant to attend the meeting. Hearing this, DiAngelo requested that the white people in the audience refrain from shedding tears while the meeting takes place. Not long after, one of the white participants angrily questioned why she was not permitted to cry—especially before the eyes of people of color.

While emotions are automatically deemed as a natural response, the truth is emotions can also be used as a political tool. Aside from emotional stresses, the tears of an individual can also be influenced by their personal beliefs, cultural upbringings and prejudices. Women also tend to cry more frequently than men do. Not to mention, white people are blinded by the assumption that evil individuals are the only ones capable of being racist.

As such, it is not surprising that white and black men would run to the rescue of a crying white woman. When white tears are shed in a multicultural setting, the people of color who are the true victims of racism are instantly forgotten. The spotlight shifts to the white woman, and the individual who has pointed out her racially biased acts or words is now the antagonist.

In the eyes of people of color, a white woman's tears in a cross-cultural setting are solid evidence of racial insulation. After all, how can white tears symbolize harmony between whites and people of color if they seldom form authentic interactions with people of color? White women in a cross-cultural setup often presume her feelings will be shared and sympathized with by people of color.

The book's author stresses that white tears are narcissistic in nature. The tears of white women are the product of the inner guilt they are experiencing. She recalls a situation where a white woman was promoted and assigned to oversee an organization that mainly deals with justice involving race. Although the women of color had significantly more experience and knowledge than the white woman, they were immediately ignored. They were even the ones who trained the white woman. The latter sought the people's support while she shed her tears. All this took place without the white woman realizing that her tears concealed the reality that racism was just strengthened by an organization meant to uphold justice among races.

CHAPTER 12: DECONSTRUCTING THE SYSTEM OF RACISM – WHERE DO WE START?

DiAngelo, together with her team, had a meeting with a web developer. The web developer happened to be black. Also included in the author's team were two black women. DiAngelo insisted that she explain herself verbally while the survey forms were being distributed by the web developer. While the meeting took place, DiAngelo elaborated on an incident where a black colleague of hers suffered discrimination. She adds that the discrimination occurred during a training session for antiracism.

The author added a joke, saying that the white people were scared by the braids of her colleagues.

After the discussion, DiAngelo was approached and informed that her joke about braids offended the web developer. The author then had a consultation with a white friend before she talked privately with the web developer and made amends.

White fragility is apparent in many forms. It can be evident in a person's actions, assertions, emotional responses and presumptions.

DiAngelo was able to break off her own racially offensive patterns in an effort to reconcile with the web developer. She expressed assertions, behaviors and feelings that contradict white fragility. In this manner, DiAngelo successfully shifted her personal model about race.

More specifically, below are the behavioral responses exhibited by the author in response to the situation:

- Appreciation

- Concern

- Empathy

- Modesty

In addition, the emotions she manifested include:

- Admission of guilt
- Attending
- Connecting
- Consideration

Her claims also comprised the contexts below:

- I am grateful for your constructive feedback
- There are things I need to work on myself
- I would like to focus on the message and not on the conveyer of the message
- Albeit hard to confront, this conversation is very important

There are many ways by which white people can be educated and enlightened about racism. Whites are more than welcome to create connections with people of color. However, people of color should not be made to bear the entire responsibility of teaching whites about racism. White individuals must also conduct research on their own and immerse themselves in relevant material that shows how they can put a stop to the apathy that white people are rendering to racial issues.

Another recommendation from the author is for white people to find a fellow white with whom they can disclose and sort out their own personal thoughts and emotions. When it comes to reconciling with a person of color following a racist remark or behavior that a white person exhibited, the latter should admit to their racial slurs and avoid creating excuses for themselves. Racial awareness is important. White individuals should learn how to challenge fellow whites who are prone to exuding arrogance and stubbornness in the face of a racial dispute.

In reality, majority of blacks are eager to provide feedback to white people. The problem is white people find it hard to accept feedback from their black brothers and sisters. Worse, they choose to reject the idea of owning up to their racist ways and fixing it. This is why it would be best for whites to find people of the same skin color (preferably also someone that they trust), and have this individual identify their shortcomings.

The troubles of white fragility are not a weight that people of color have to bear on their own. In fact, white people are the ones who need to be taught about racial awareness.

EDITORIAL REVIEW

The sensitive and ever-elusive topic of racial equality in the modern American setting is discussed by Robin J. DiAngelo. Her book, White Fragility, attempts to dare white people who are prone to avoid racial issues, to be more open when it comes to discussing racial equality.

The term 'White Fragility' was invented by the author in the midst of working on a peer-reviewed paper. The year was 2011. White people exhibited defensive actions whenever they find themselves caught in between a certain degree of racial stress—hence, the inspiration for the said term.

Arguing, playing the victim, turning the situation by deflecting racist accusations to the other person and walking out are some of the defense mechanisms often manifested by white people. DiAngelo specifically focuses on the misinformed racial perspective that white people have. She asserts that to a certain extent, white people are racist. This is in contrast to what white people believe: Uneducated and evil individuals are the only ones capable of becoming racist. On the other hand, DiAngelo's assertion does not imply that all white people are wicked. What she wishes to point out is that, whites have the tendency to view colored individuals as inferior to them as a result of their upbringing and social conditioning. A concrete example of this is the way a white individual expresses what appears to be a normal statement or phrase. Deep down, however, this seemingly harmless remark is actual an instigator of more stereotypes on race.

Think about how white people make use of coded remarks when describing neighborhoods that are mostly occupied by black families and individuals. They would often suggest putting off any plans of purchasing a house in a particular neighborhood. White people would even add that their friends might need a gun to protect themselves if they ever push through with buying a home in a predominantly black-inhabited part of town.

Several real-life experiences are disclosed by the author to further stress her point. She also uses her examples to underscore the fragility of whites whenever they are confronted about racial issues. Racism is, after all, a very persistent problem. When a teacher was obviously ridiculing a black parent, she was shocked and ended up having a nervous breakdown after DiAngelo pointed out her racist statement and behavior.

The overall tone of the book is casual—a detail that was particularly chosen by the author to make it easier for readers to follow White Fragility's contents. As an academic, DiAngelo is used to using terms that are complex for the general audience. Despite that, she was able to simply each of the concepts that she laid out in her book. One of the main objectives of her book is to drive both personal and national revolution. By simplifying the terms she used in White Fragility, it becomes easier for readers to relate to her and understand her explanations. The more people are able to come into terms with the facts and ideas presented in the book, the more likely DiAngelo is able to fulfill her purpose.

There have also been other authors who have tackled racial issues in the past. Eduardo Bonilla-Silva, Omowale Akintunde and Ta-Nehisi Coates are just some of the many authors who have published written works about racism. DiAngelo has included and referenced the works of these authors.

What sets White Fragility apart from previously published books about racism is how DiAngelo was able to point out white supremacy as a crucial factor in strengthening racial bias in today's society. Her distinct perspective on racism stems from the reality that she is a white person who carries years of experience spreading knowledge about social justice and racial issues. Her views are not entirely personal opinions. She combines her own upbringing with her social experiences to exhibit just how much of a structural and systemic hurdle racism is in America.

White Fragility is not the author's initial attempt at writing about racial discrimination in the U.S. Prior to publishing this book, she has worked on two other books that discuss the following topics: (1) How white people can enhance their racial literacy; and (2) Social justice. The purpose of DiAngelo is to provide fellow whites with concrete examples of how white fragility continues to feed racism in the society. White people can contribute to the demolishment of the existing racial structure. By choosing to take part in constructive discussions with fellow whites and people of color they begin to realize that running away from the issue at hand only makes them an accomplice to the growing racial division around them.

Thank you for taking time to buy and read this book. We hope you enjoyed or learned something from it. If you find this summary interesting, please purchase and read the original book for full content experience!

We would highly appreciate it if you post a good review and share it to your family and friends and other like-minded individuals.

To Good Life,

Goldmine Reads

BOOKS THAT YOU MAY ALSO ENJOY

Look for these book Titles by Goldmine Reads. Available in various stores and formats.

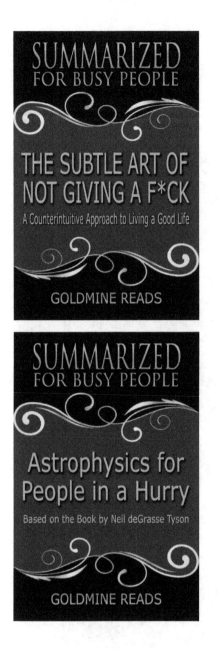

SUMMARIZED
FOR BUSY PEOPLE

THE SUBTLE ART OF
NOT GIVING A F*CK
A Counterintuitive Approach to Living a Good Life

GOLDMINE READS

SUMMARIZED
FOR BUSY PEOPLE

SAPIENS
A Brief History of Humankind

GOLDMINE READS

SUMMARIZED
FOR BUSY PEOPLE

Astrophysics for
People in a Hurry
Based on the Book by Neil deGrasse Tyson

GOLDMINE READS

SUMMARIZED
FOR BUSY PEOPLE

WHEAT
BELLY
Lose the Wheat, Lose the Weight,
and Find Your Path Back to Health

GOLDMINE READS

SUMMARIZED
FOR BUSY PEOPLE

LEONARDO
DA VINCI

Based on the Book by Walter Isaacson

GOLDMINE READS

SUMMARIZED
FOR BUSY PEOPLE

THE BOOK
OF JOY

Lasting Happiness in a Changing World

GOLDMINE READS

SUMMARIZED
FOR BUSY PEOPLE

EXTREME
OWNERSHIP

How U.S. Navy SEALs Lead and Win

GOLDMINE READS

SUMMARIZED
FOR BUSY PEOPLE

EMOTIONAL
INTELLIGENCE
2.0

Based on the Book by Travis Bradberry

GOLDMINE READS

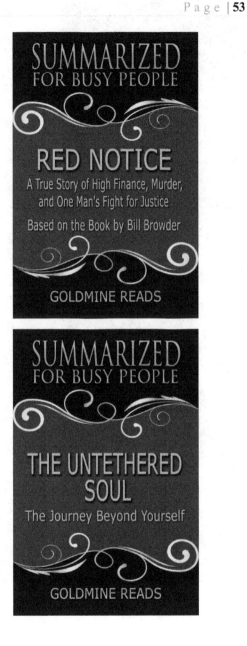

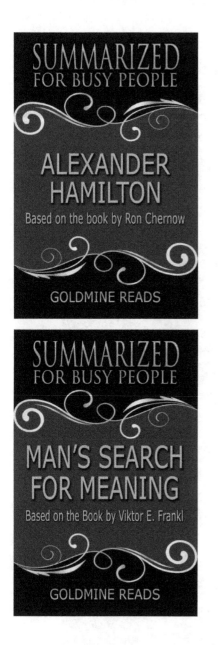

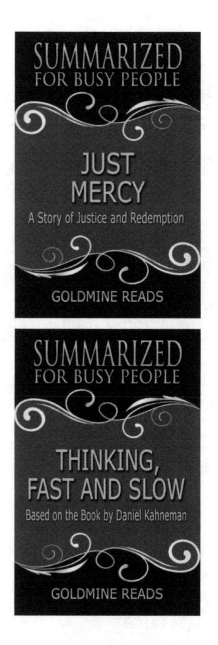

SUMMARIZED
FOR BUSY PEOPLE

GRIT

The Power of Passion and Perseverance

Based on the Book by Angela Duckworth

GOLDMINE READS

SUMMARIZED
FOR BUSY PEOPLE

QUIET

The Power of Introverts in a
World That Can't Stop Talking

Based on the Book by Susan Cain

GOLDMINE READS

SUMMARIZED
FOR BUSY PEOPLE

THE POWER
OF HABIT

Why We Do What We Do In Life and Business

Based on the Book by Charles Duhigg

GOLDMINE READS

SUMMARIZED
FOR BUSY PEOPLE

HOMO DEUS

A Brief History of Tomorrow

Based on the Book by Yuval Noah Harari

GOLDMINE READS

SUMMARIZED
FOR BUSY PEOPLE

EVERYBODY,
ALWAYS

Becoming Love in a World Full of Setbacks and Difficult People

Based on the Book by Bob Goff

GOLDMINE READS

SUMMARIZED
FOR BUSY PEOPLE

THE BODY KEEPS
THE SCORE

Brain, Mind, and Body in the Healing of Trauma

Based on the Book by Bessel van der Kolk MD

GOLDMINE READS

SUMMARIZED
FOR BUSY PEOPLE

THE MIRACLE
MORNING

The Not-So-Obvious Secret Guaranteed
to Transform Your Life (Before 8AM)

GOLDMINE READS

SUMMARIZED
FOR BUSY PEOPLE

THE COMPLETE GUIDE
TO FASTING

Heal Your Body Through Intermittent,
Alternate-Day, and Extended Fasting

GOLDMINE READS

SUMMARIZED
FOR BUSY PEOPLE

FEAR
Trump in the White House

Based on the Book by Bob Woodward

GOLDMINE READS

SUMMARIZED
FOR BUSY PEOPLE

GIRL, WASH
YOUR FACE
Stop Believing the Lies About Who You Are
So You Can Become Who You Were Meant to Be

GOLDMINE READS

SUMMARIZED
FOR BUSY PEOPLE

21 LESSONS FOR
THE 21st CENTURY

Based on the Book by Yuval Noah Harari

GOLDMINE READS

SUMMARIZED
FOR BUSY PEOPLE

BAD BLOOD
Secrets and Lies in a Silicon Valley Startup

Based on the Book by John Carreyrou

GOLDMINE READS

SUMMARIZED
FOR BUSY PEOPLE

START
WITH WHY
How Great Leaders Inspire Everyone to Take Action
Based on the Book by Simon Sinek

GOLDMINE READS

SUMMARIZED
FOR BUSY PEOPLE

GIRL, STOP
APOLOGIZING
A Shame-Free Plan for Embracing
and Achieving Your Goals

GOLDMINE READS

SUMMARIZED
FOR BUSY PEOPLE

THE GIFTS OF
IMPERFECTION
Let Go of Who You Think You're Supposed
to Be and Embrace Who You Are

GOLDMINE READS

SUMMARIZED
FOR BUSY PEOPLE

DIGITAL
MINIMALISM
Choosing a Focused Life in a Noisy World
Based on the Book by Cal Newport

GOLDMINE READS

SUMMARIZED
FOR BUSY PEOPLE

MEASURE
WHAT MATTERS

How Google, Bono, and the Gates
Foundation Rock the World with OKRs

GOLDMINE READS

SUMMARIZED
FOR BUSY PEOPLE

THE CHECKLIST
MANIFESTO

How to Get Things Right

Based on the Book by Atul Gawande

GOLDMINE READS

SUMMARIZED
FOR BUSY PEOPLE

ENLIGHTENMENT
NOW

The Case for Reason, Science, Humanism, and Progress

Based on the Book by Steven Pinker

GOLDMINE READS

SUMMARIZED
FOR BUSY PEOPLE

ATTACHED

The New Science of Adult Attachment and
How It Can Help You Find—and Keep—Love

Based on the Book by Amir Levine

GOLDMINE READS

CPSIA information can be obtained
at www.ICGtesting.com
Printed in the USA
LVHW021611120620
657940LV00019B/3335